The Learn

For a complete list of Management Books 2000 titles
visit our web-site on http://www.mb2000.com

Other books in this series include:

The Communication Toolkit
The Customer Service Toolkit
The Developing People Toolkit
The Human Resources Toolkit
The Motivation Toolkit
The Systems Thinking Toolkit
The Team Management Toolkit

The Learning Toolkit

Practical ways to improve personal and work performance

Stuart Emmett

This book is dedicated to my family – to my wife, the lovely Christine, to our two cute children, Jill and James, and James's wife, Mairead (also cute), and to our totally gorgeous three granddaughters, twins Megan and Molly and their younger sister, Niamh.

First published in 2008 by Management Books 2000 Ltd
Forge House, Limes Road
Kemble, Cirencester
Gloucestershire, GL7 6AD, UK
Tel: 0044 (0) 1285 771441
Fax: 0044 (0) 1285 771055
Email: info@mb2000.com
Web: www.mb2000.com

British Library Cataloguing in Publication Data is available

ISBN 9781852525620

Contents

About this book

In writing this book, I have made best-efforts endeavours not to include anything that, if used, would be injurious or cause financial loss to the user. The user is, however, strongly recommended, before applying or using any of the contents, to check and verify their own company policy/requirements. No liability will be accepted for the use of any of the contents.

It can also happen in a lifetime of learning and meeting people, that the original source of an idea or information has been forgotten. If I have actually omitted in this book to give anyone credit they are due, I do apologise and hope they will make contact so I can correct the omission in future editions.

About the author

My own journey to "today", whilst an individual one, did not happen, thankfully, without other peoples involvement. I smile when I remember so many helpful people. So to anyone who has ever had contact with me, then please be assured you will have contributed to my own learning, growing and developing.

After spending over 30 years in commercial private sector service industries, I entered the logistics and supply chain people development business. After nine years as a Director of Training, I then choose to become a freelance independent mentor/coach, trainer and consultant. This built on my past operational and strategic experience - gained in the UK and Nigeria - and my particular interest in the "people issues" of management processes.

Trading under the name of Learn and Change Limited, I currently enjoy working all over the UK and also on four other continents, principally in Africa and the Middle East, but also in the Far East and South America. In addition to my training activities, I am also involved in one-to-one coaching/mentoring, consulting, writing, assessing and examining for professional institutes' and university qualifications.

I can be contacted at stuart@learnandchange.com or by visiting www.learnandchange.com. I welcome any comments.

Introduction

Welcome to this new series of business toolkits designed to improve personal and work performance.

A recent report entitled "The Missing Millions – how companies mismanage their most valuable resource" (source: www.Proudfootconsulting.com) stated that "Poor management in the UK is directly responsible for 60 lost working days per employee per year. And a further 25 days lost annually can also be indirectly attributed to management failing."

That is a total of 85 wasted days per employee every year due to poor and failing management. This is around 30% of a normal working year of 240 available days!

According to the report, the main contributing factors were as follows:

- Insufficient planning and control
- Inadequate supervision
- Poor morale
- Inappropriate people development
- IT related problems
- Ineffective communication

This series of concise guides will provide practical advice in each of these key management areas, to enable managers to get the most out of their teams, and make sure that they stay ahead of the game.

The simple truth is that in order to avoid the incredible 85 wasted days per employee per year referred to above, things must be done better *by management.*

Problems with management will almost always turn out to be people problems. Improving performance is therefore essentially about improving individual and team performance so that, in turn, the organisation's performance is improved.

This will require that, for example, the following are considered:

- Developing a strong strategic vision that is underpinned with learning
- Motivating and developing and releasing the potential of people, as individuals and in teams
- Communicating to people what is expected, what they are rewarded for, how they should deliver results and what results the organisation is looking for.

The earlier mentioned Proudfoot research highlighted several areas that managers can work on to improve performance. These are shown again below with a link to the appropriate Toolkit:

- Insufficient planning and control – see the Systems Thinking Toolkit
- Inadequate supervision – see the Team Management Toolkit
- Poor morale – see the Motivation Toolkit
- Inappropriate people development – see the Developing People Toolkit
- IT related problems – see the Systems Thinking Toolkit
- Ineffective communication – see the Communication Toolkit

It should be appreciated that many of these aspects do inter-relate, and that a single quick fix in one area may not always work very well. The Systems Thinking Toolkit does examine more fully all of the interconnected links of inputs, processes and outputs to be considered when improving performance.

As we have seen, many of the Proudfoot research aspects are directly people-related. In addition to the specific toolkits mentioned above, the Human Resources Toolkit provides a complete framework for effective human resources management.

Finally, as we all know, no business can survive without customers, and the essential skills of customer service are absolutely vital to the retention and growth of the customer base. The Customer Service Toolkit provides quick and easy advice which will produce startling returns.

All of these toolkits are designed to assist readers to implement change in their businesses. However, to implement change effectively, this requires new learning, both by the manager seeking to implement the change, and also by the staff who are expected to take on board the new processes and to learn and develop the associated skills. In this respect the Learning Toolkit is perhaps the most important of all the toolkits – the skills and processes set out in this book are of paramount importance to the entire series.

Part 1. The Importance of Learning

"Those who are in love with learning are in love with life" (Charles Handy)

"Learning is more important than knowledge" (Einstein)

"All experience is learning" (Peter Vaill)

"In times of change, it the learners that inherit the future" (Stuart Emmett)

Just about everything we ever do must be learnt. However, learning is not an automatic process; it is a skill. Yet how many of us, after having committed ourselves to learn, have nevertheless failed to consider *how* we can learn *better*. Many people have no idea how they "learn"; they consider it all to be just plain common sense. Many others will only learn by "accident" and unconsciously. Whilst this is one way of learning, just think how much more could actually be learnt by actively learning how to learn better?

This toolkit will provide you with checklists and fact files to enable you to better consider how to learn and maximise your learning experiences.

What is learning?

Learning is fundamentally about thinking and doing something new. Consider the following definition:

"Learning is the process by which you use your personal knowledge and experience to enable you to:

- *Make sense of things, by thinking*
- *Make things happen, by doing*
- *Bring about change, by moving from one position to another"*

Learning, therefore, is essentially: "I think – I do – I move".

Learning is a source of change. When people learn, their behaviour, defined here as simply what is said and or done, will change.

When people are at the advanced stage of "wanting to continually learn," they will actually demand learning and will seek it out in all situations.

Why Learn?

Different people will have different answers to this question. The answers may well include some of the following:

- To acquire knowledge.
- To gain a qualification.
- To develop skills.
- To grow and develop myself.
- To understand a subject better.
- To keep up with changes.
- To make sense of new ideas.
- Because you have been told to.
- To get a better job/employment.
- To create my own future.
- To get nearer to what I want to be.

Whatever your reason for learning, in order for it to be successful you need to "buy into" the process. You really do have to be committed to learn. You have to want to do it. Learning is the ultimate DIY process.

Learning ultimately depends on individual responsibility. A strong sense of ownership of the process is essential.

Action time - why learn?

Ask yourself the following questions - please write down your answers:

- Why do I want to learn?
- What do I want to learn?
- What outcome do I want?
- Do I know anyone else who has done something similar?
- Who can help me decide?
- What level of time and money commitment will I have to make?
- What effect will this commitment have on my life at home and on my work?
- Am I sure I am really prepared to make this commitment?

Part 2. The Learning Process

It is both useful and important in learning to have a healthy curiosity about the unique way that we personally learn.

Whilst "our way" will be unique to us, we will all go through the following stages:

- Motivation, by deciding "what is in it for me" (WIIFM)
- Obtain data and facts
- Convert this to information
- Get insight and hopefully an "aha" moment
- This will give us knowledge, or "know-how"
- When this is used, we develop skills
- At each stage, we need to Reflect and Revise

So we start with motivation and pass through the subsequent stages. Another view of these stages follows:

- Motivation is "I Will"
- Knowledge is "I Know"
- Doing is "I Do"
- Skills is "I Can Do"

Reflecting and revising is done at the "end" of learning, when we start again with the next learning.

Learning and Motivation

Motivation is a key aspect in learning. Motivation occurs in a number of different ways and on a number of different levels, as illustrated in the following diagram (see the Motivation Toolkit for a fuller explanation):

Motivation Levels (Source: after Maslow, Covey)

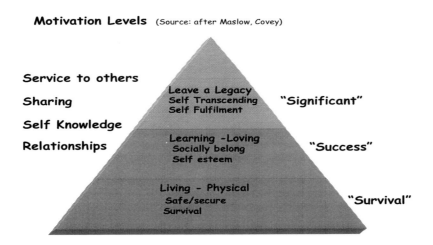

The levels of motivation vary for different people. Some may need to learn for survival and living, others for personal success and others to fulfil themselves.

17

Basic Requirements for Learning

The basic requirements for learning can be described as follows:

1) Learning, in the final analysis, is your responsibility. You need to have the sense of ownership and commitment. Learning is really voluntary. It is your unique and personal journey.

2) Learning is a skill that develops new behaviour. Attending a training course is not in itself learning. It is only in the application and in the doing that learning happens. Learning involves new skills and new behaviour. This can involve experimenting, taking risks and making mistakes. All of these provide learning experiences.

3) Learning requires continual feedback. We need feedback from others to help us understand ourselves and what we do. Learning is harder without such feedback. Many of us aren't aware of what we need to learn. The gaps in our knowledge and experience may not always be obvious to us. Feedback indicates how far we are on or off the track, so that we can make the necessary adjustments – and learn.

4) Learning is a process not an outcome. With the pace of life, work, and continual change, we will need to set ourselves realistic and attainable objectives and targets. We need to see these objectives as milestones along the road of development not as just an end in themselves. When you are through learning then you are through!

5) Learning is a total involvement. Our personal development and professional development are related. The technical aspects of work issues are important, but so also are the people management issues. The people issues require us to review our relationships at both work and home. True learning looks at all aspects of our lives.

Learning to Learn is a fundamental part of developing as an individual. When people effectively learn to learn, they then have a different view of themselves. Self-confidence is enhanced. They are able to deal better with change. Indeed they will now embrace change opportunities.

Never, however, confuse attending a training course with learning. You will not automatically learn anything from school, college, university or from a training course. Consider the following differences between training and learning:

Teaching is	Learning is
Done to you/Passive	Done to self/Active
Dependent on others	Can create own ways
Formal	Formal and informal
Delivered at fixed times	Undertaken in discretionary time
Externally motivated	Internally motivated
"Proving"	"Improving" continuously
Objectives & ends are given	Objectives are subjectively determined
Outcomes-driven	Process-driven
Gives solutions	Solving problems

The Learning Process of a Child

As a child you learnt to walk by being encouraged and supported (physically as well as mentally). Our early learning was better facilitated in comfortable surroundings with a friendly atmosphere.

In summary, the learning process of a child involves:

- Encouragement
- Support
- Friendly atmosphere
- Comfortable surrounding

The key points here are that the learning style is holistic, exploratory, emotional and logical.

These "external-to-the-learner" conditions are critical to the largely open learning process of a child. Unfortunately, many adults have become closed to learning. In doing so they have forgotten the excellent role model of children learning.

The Learning Process As We Get Older

It is often said that we start to get "closed down" at school. Here we meet and interact with strangers. There may be some embarrassment. Our confidence may be shaken and we can develop self-doubt. Others' viewpoints, differences and experiences may run counter to our "world view". Group views take precedence and the learning style used will be more structured, linear, rigid and conforming. Logic and rationality now tend to override emotional feelings.

Our earlier, more single and (for us) positive view is now challenged by group views. Such a forced and structured learning style in formalised education may well close us down to learning.

Negative instruction can also affect us at home – consider the effect of admonishments like "who do you think you are?", "that's too good for you", "I want never gets", etc. These run counter to encouragement and support and can remain deeply etched in the memory, projected through our subconscious mind influencing how we experience the world and ourselves.

This can further exacerbate the change from our very early holistic style of learning towards a structured, linear and rigid approach where, as mentioned above, we conform to "group" views and the views of "significant others". We have been conditioned to become "single track" learners.

These group and others' views can separate us from and run counter to our needs for:

- individual emotional health
- feelings of physical safety
- believing we are a good role model to ourselves.

These needs provide us with positive stimulus for our self-esteem and self-worth. Such emotional feelings are important to our learning as they can influence our behaviour and drive our motivation. But because our emotions are often never really understood or accounted for by others, many of the people involved in our learning processes will totally ignore our emotional needs.

This may, in part, be because emotions cannot be measured in the same way as writing, reading, spelling and arithmetic; whilst the latter will be measured and controlled at school, our emotional needs are so often neglected.

The solution is to take charge of our own learning experiences and to make them apply to specifically to our own personal and emotional needs. We will show later how to do this after we consider some theoretical aspects of learning.

Learning Theory

Understandably this has received some attention over the years. A summary of the major learning theories follows. Some of these have been around for some time, but in more recent times we have discovered much more about how our brains operate. Indeed it has been said that we have learnt more about the human brain in the last two decades than in man's total existence. So, of course, those who undertook their early learning before the 1980s may not have benefited from these newer views.

Behaviourist theories

- Fundamentally about stick-and-carrot reinforcement
- Main method: verbal instruction from an "expert" who may also support and guide

Cognitive theories

- Information processing and comparison to mental models to give understanding and knowledge.
- Main method: facilitation on the "content" e.g. by case study, best practice

Constructivist theories

- Personal knowledge, in context.
- Main method: participating/reflecting by the learner.

Social Practice theories

- Supports all the previous three, but these must be applied in a social setting.
- Main method: networking, participation in communities/teams, etc.

The following mental models can be found:

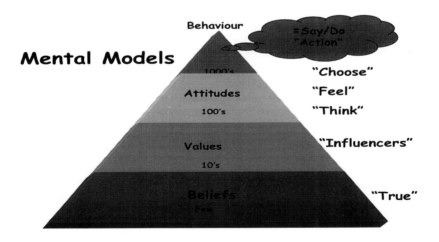

At the core of behaviour are beliefs, those essential truths that human beings hold. These few beliefs will drive our values; in turn these will influence our thinking and feelings and give us our attitudes. These operate automatically as a filter through which we make decisions and choose what we will say or what we will do. This then becomes our externally visible behaviour.

Our behaviour is therefore a visible and external expression of our more invisible and internal beliefs, values and attitudes. Behaviour that is automatically repeated, usually unconsciously, becomes habit.

To change a habit will often involve more than a behaviour change; it will more likely require a change to the attitudes that cause the behaviour. For a deep-rooted habit, then clearly the deeper underpinning values and beliefs may also have to be changed.

Driving a car is a habit for most of us. When we started out learning to drive, we believed we could do it and the instructor's help and the sight of others driving reinforced our belief. Eventually we passed the driving test and then we continued the learning process "on the job" (i.e. by driving). Eventually, we became able to drive without really thinking about it, while listening to the radio, or talking to passengers.

Here then, is a classic illustration, of taking an initial consciously made belief and turning it into an unconscious habit.

This can also be seen in operation in the UK every year at New Year's Resolution time, with the ever-popular resolutions to lose weight or to quit smoking. At this time the desire to lose weight, for example, is reinforced by the advertising campaigns of gyms that endeavour to get people signed up for a year's membership. Gyms are at their busiest in January – but by February/March they have returned towards to their pre-Christmas attendances, as the majority of people have reverted back to their former habits.

Those really committed people will, however, continue. The key word here is "commitment", as it will be this commitment to a deeper set of values or beliefs which has actually overcome the more superficial attitudes and behaviour. This commitment has been made consciously and will need to be continually reinforced; then, and only then, will it work upwards via attitudes and eventually become an unconscious but a new pattern of behaviour.

With the New Year's Resolutions about quitting smoking, an identical pattern follows. In January we see a rush of advertising for anti-smoking patches and chewing gums and the Government "stop smoking" campaigns. The advertisements tail off in February, as by then many people have followed the similar patterns explained above and reverted back to their former habits (reinforced by the effects of the nicotine drug). Only those who really believed in giving up smoking have a chance of success.

Beliefs are therefore a core and vital part of our "make-up". They can and they do change lives. Learning continually is a useful belief to have. To summarise:

- Behaviour is "what we say or do"
- Attitudes are the "way we see and think about things"
- Beliefs/Values are "what we know to be true"
- Habits represent repeated and learned behaviour, (so to change the habit you have to change the attitude that creates it).

Part 3. Integrating Learning

The following mind map gives an overview of the approach used in this toolkit. We have already started discussing nurture and shall be discussing each other topic further:

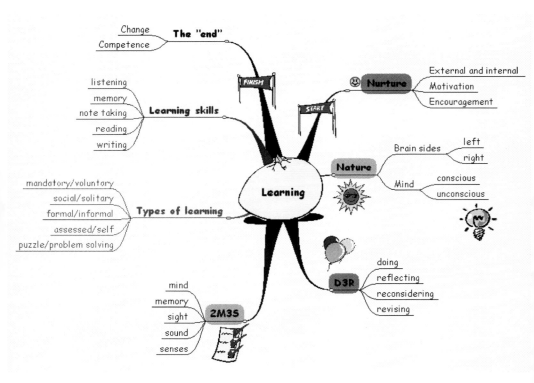

We can also see these connections in the following feedback loop model:

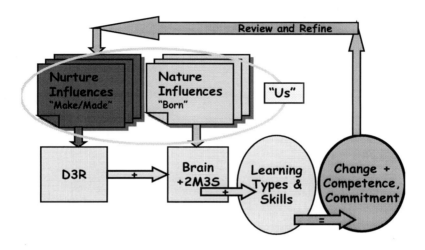

Nature or Nurture Influences?

This is a perennial debate – which has the strongest influence? Is personality innate or are we shaped by our upbringing and environmental pressures? An analogy: nature "loads the gun" whilst it is our nurture that "presses the trigger". To amplify these influences further we can see that:

- Nature is within us; it is what we are born with – for example, our brain that covers aspects like mind, memory, sight, sound and senses.
- Nurture relates to our socialisation process – for example, how we are brought up – and includes things like

encouragement and support. It is therefore partly internal – for example, how we choose to think about something – and is also partly external – for example, the source of the encouragement. We can of course choose to give ourselves self-encouragement! As we have already seen above, nurture can have a direct impact on our learning styles.

Whilst there is no real evidence to determine whether nature or nurture is the stronger influence with learning, my guess would be 33% nature and 66% nurture.

In any event, whilst we can obviously not influence our nature or what we are born with, we can certainly influence the "nurture" element.

The Learning Jigsaw

It is important to appreciate the way that we naturally prefer to learn. People will only learn if they want to. They learn in different ways. They have their own preferences, as well as having different levels of competence and commitment – competence being the knowledge and skills required to do something, the "know-how", and commitment being the confidence and motivation to do it.

Learning is a cyclical and spiralling process. The stages in the so-called "D3R" cycle are:

1. Doing
2. Reflecting
3. Reconstructing
4. Revising

We must go through all these stages at some time in our learning. However, because of our personal preferences and personality, we may prefer some stages more than others. For example, a task-orientated "gets-things-done" person will prefer more hands-on doing, than spending time on reflecting.

However we do need all stages when learning. They are like parts of a jigsaw; all must fit together so we can then benefit from the overall picture.

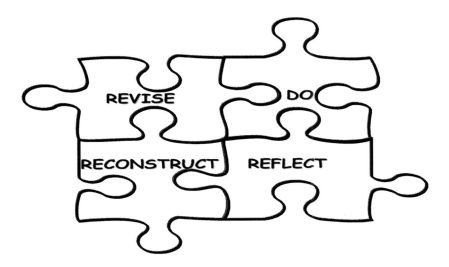

Doing

We start our learning process by gaining experience through undertaking an activity; we "do" something. This can involve the following:

- Experiencing
- Exploring
- Performing
- Trying
- Being Active
- "Hands-on" learning

Key point: Get a better **"Awareness"** about something.

Reflecting

We then think on this experience and attempt to understand it through analysis and conceptualisation; we "reflect" and "think".

- Getting feedback
- "Tell-me" learners
- Reviewing
- Reasoning
- Evaluating
- Conceptualising

Key point here is: **"Thinking"**. Most people will rush or ignore this stage; it should not be!

Reconsidering

Next, we make choices based on analysing the implications of alternative options; we "reconsider and reconstruct."

- Reconstructing
- Realising
- Connecting
- Implications of alternatives
- Concluding

Key point: **"Understanding"** and **"Know-how"**

Revising

Then, we decide on the next steps to take; we "revise" or change our behaviour.

- Refining
- Planning
- Committing
- Deciding on the next steps

Key Point: Determining **"how to"** and a Commitment to **"do"**

Then the cycle starts again with a new experience and a new awareness – providing of course, that we continue, to be motivated to learn.

Thereafter we undergo another experience, and we "do" something again, but differently and better – then it is reflected upon again, reconsidered and reconstructed, and a revised way to do it results.

All of this process can be undertaken with help and feedback from others. It is a process that is also constantly repeated. It is a learning spiral of doing – reflecting – reconsidering and reconstructing - revising – doing – reflecting – reconsidering and reconstructing – revising – doing, and so on.

Varied ways round the spiral

There are various ways that we can pass round the learning spiral:

Single loop or adaptive learning (e.g. trial and error; learning by rote)	Double loop or generative learning (e.g. see or do it differently)
Fixed mental model	Changed mental model
Used for skills development and in improving our existing mental models	Used for renewing and changing our perspectives and mental models
In stable and fixed situations	In turbulent and dynamic situations
"Puzzle-solving" with a fixed answer	"Problem-solving" with uncertain outcomes and possible "paradox"

Learning is therefore a cyclical and a never-ending spiral. It is almost automatic. However, actually believing that it is automatic and unconscious is dangerous. To learn better, people need to *consciously* think about how to learn.

Learning is certainly a natural process. Maybe having to learn about how to learn is the unnatural process. Learning how to learn (L2L) has to be a conscious process that, hopefully, will then become a natural process!

There are many learning "nature" influences and these largely involve our brain, the B+2M+3S in our mind map:

- **B**=Brain sides : Logical left and creative right
- **M** =Mind : Conscious and unconscious
- **M** =Memory : Short-working-long terms
- **3S**: Sight-sound-senses

The Influence of Our Brain

We use our senses to gather information from the outside world. The ears (sound/hearing), eyes (sight/seeing), and sense of movement/touch (sensing), all send in different signals. It is in the way that the signals are combined, that a permanent impression is made on the brain.

Exposure to new material should not be mistaken with learning it. For example, we never learnt to drive a car by reading or watching. To learn we need to push ourselves to be actively involved by doing something (e.g. driving the car). This, essentially, is the only way to learn.

For example:

- **When listening** – take notes, draw diagrams, ask questions (especially "Why?" questions), volunteer to participate. Afterwards recite key points to yourself, review your notes with any text and above all push yourself to be active.

- **When reading** – take notes, draw diagrams, read difficult material out loud. If it is instructional material, do the exercise or activity now. Read and do. Do and push yourself to be active.

Remember also that we use both conscious and unconscious parts of our brain. For example, some situations require a clear and logical thought process. Other situations may call for a more creative and open style. We may tend unconsciously to be more active/impulsive. We may not "like" being reflective and thoughtful.

The main point to be appreciated here is that if we stay only on one style then we may miss the other ways. It is surely better to apply the whole self to your learning?

Left and right brain divisions

As everyone knows, our brain is in composed of two halves, the left hemisphere and the right hemisphere. At least, this is the simple view. Front and back, upper and lower quadrants are other "divisions". Research into brain activity, continues to contribute to our understanding at a rapid pace.

In terms of "left" and "right", it is generally recognised that we have a logical left-side brain and a creative right-side brain. The left-side brain will firstly conduct an Analysis, will then Act, and finally will Feel, (for example, is the action "correct" and "right"?). The right-side brain however, works the other way round: Feeling, then Action, then Analysis.

The following brain division can be seen:

Logical left brain

- Think/Analyse, Act, Feel
- Convergent "head" thinker, then "do"
- Prefer written, mathematical, science-based approaches

- Objective, linear thinking , short term views
- Analytical step-by-step head thinkers
- Rational facts-based reasoning that converges

Creative right brain

- Feel, Think/Analyse, Act
- Divergent "heart" feeler/thinker, then "do"
- Prefer musical, artistic and visual-based approaches
- Subjective, parallel processing, longer-term views
- Creative, free-flowing "heart" thinkers
- Emotional feelings with synthesis that diverges

Note: The brain likes: water, oxygen, laughter, movement, challenge, change, protein and vitamins. Unsurprisingly it does not like the opposites!

The following widens this "ideal-typical view" of the brain

Logical left brain	Creative right brain
Written	Spoken
Mathematical	Musical
Science	Art
Objective	Subjective
Linear/parts	Holistic/Wholes
Analytical	Creative
Step by step	Free flowing
"Thinker"	"Feeler"

Convergent	Divergent
Reactive	Adaptive
Rational	Emotional
Self reliant "me"	Group orientation "we"
Rational	Emotional
Hearing	Verbal/Visual
"Head" thinker	"Heart" thinker
Concrete things	Abstract emotions
Facts	Feelings
Shorter term views	Longer term view
Analyse-act-feel	**Feel-analyse-act**

You will see the brain division goes into many aspects of our total "make-up" and personality.

The brain is better designed than any machine. Its power and capacity is increased or decreased by the use we make of it. The brain is like a muscle that can be exercised so that not only does it maintain itself, but it also improves, develops, and does new things. Just as physical exercise will maintain and improve muscle power, so learning to learn will maintain, and improve the brainpower. This means people can extend their personal capacity and performance.

Individuals will tend to be more comfortable using one or other of the brain sides, and their thinking styles will tend instinctively to favour that particular side – which means they can miss out on the other side. However, to be complete, we need to use *both* sides – known as "whole brain thinking".

Our brain is actually very similar to everyone else's. The difference comes from how we use it.

Ways of learning differ and people will react differently to different styles. As far as the brain is concerned, using it is important:

- **Absorbing** needs to use both sides
- **Retaining** needs use both sides
- Then we are better able to:
  - make connections
  - reflect wider
  - review all
  - make more connections and so on

We can think of the brain as a coin that demonstrates its full value from both of its sides not just one. Thinking of the brain like this and trying to use both sides will help to ensure that we continually use more than only one half of our brainpower.

We do need to appreciate which side we are on and then recognise how this fits to our current work and with our past. It is then useful to recognise that the other side may help us to learn better and then we can try doing some "opposite" brain activities.

To "force" yourself to use both sides of the brain, have a look at the following:

Action time - Brain Sides: Which side are you?

If you are more on the right side, then you need to try to develop your logical left-brain thinking. You could try the following:

- Practice and plan a step-by-step approach to learning
- Time plan each step
- Make lists of what needs to be done
- Order and structure your work space
- Set deadlines and force yourself to follow them

or, more generally:
- Discover how a machine works.
- Be on time for appointments.
- Run a personal computer.
- Analyse a problem into its main parts.

If you are more on the left side, then you need to try to develop your creative right-brain thinking. You could try the following:

- Brainstorm to create ideas
- Make visual mind-map notes to enable free-flowing visual images
- Try something new and different such as learning to play the piano
- Break your routine by studying in a new place
- Use all your five senses

or, more generally:
- Try and understand your pet's feelings.
- Create your personal logo.
- Drive to "no where".
- Explore a new neighbourhood.

The real trick to developing ourselves therefore, is to force ourselves to use the style we are less comfortable with. Remember we need to push ourselves to be active.

The Mind and the Memory

The mind is a part of the brain and has active/conscious and unconscious/background parts as follows:

Conscious mind

- Bit at a time, Parts to whole,
- Objective, Serial function,
- "Right/wrong"
- Active and controlling

Unconscious mind

- Big picture, Whole to parts
- Subjective, Parallel functions,
- Errors are learning lessons
- Receptive and participatory

Processing occurs in the memory as follows:

- First into the Short-term memory, therefore we need to ensure that we do rote/quick repeats/reviews at least three times.
- Next into the Working memory, therefore we need to deduce/think/reflect
- Finally, into Long-term memory, where the memory works on two levels:

- *Conscious*, reflecting what we are currently experiencing from doing and during "learning"
- *Unconscious*, when it becomes a habit, a skill and has been "learnt"

Reflecting and reviewing are therefore important steps to facilitate the progression from the short to the long-term/unconscious memory.

The Influence of Our Senses

Remember that how people perceive a thing is very real to them – "Perception is Reality". But it may not be real to others. We can think differently as a result of the way our brain organises and processes information. This is normal.

However recognising and accepting that we think differently can dramatically change the way we react and deal with other people. For example, we can then be more understanding and considerate of others viewpoints.

We perceive reality by seeing (sight), hearing (sound) or sensing (touch-taste-smell-physical feelings), i.e. the visual seeing and looking, the auditory hearing sounds and the kinaesthetic (the moving/touching/physical) activities. These can have powerful impacts for us.

We "take in" data and receive feedback as follows:

- *Sound-hearing*. Sounds are remembered – for example, "I hear what you're saying"
- *Sight-visual*. Pictures are remembered – for example, "I get the picture"

- *Senses –kinaesthetic.* Touch/taste/smell/"feelings" are remembered – for example, "That touches a raw nerve"

However, the strength of memory through the senses is hierarchical, as reflected in the following Chinese Proverb:

"I hear and I forget, I see and I might remember, but when I do, then I understand."

It is said that we remember:

- 20% of what we hear (Sound)
- 30% of what we see (Sight)
- 50% of what we hear and see,
- 80% of what we hear, see and do (Sight, sound, senses)

The aim therefore is to try and use all of the senses.

The following exercise will illustrate this further:

SSS (sight, sounds, senses) and memory

Sight/Visual

Think of a picture which, when seen today, takes you back and gives you a pleasant memory.

Sounds/Hearing

Think of a sound, perhaps musical, which, when heard today, takes you back to a pleasant memory?

Senses/Kinaesthetic

Think of a physical sensation (touch, taste or smell), physical feeling), which, when repeated today, takes you back to a pleasant memory?

Which of these three types of trigger has the strongest memory associations for you?

The point here is the way that these triggers act on us, because we have locked away SSS stimuli. The taking in, unconsciously, of "reality" via SSS preferences is very powerful.

We can also decide consciously, to lock away new triggers, for future recall as we move towards the future we have planned.

It is usually the case that a group of people will express different SSS preferences, some responding more strongly to pictures, some to sounds, and some to physical sensation. Research into this area is continually being developed but so far it would seem that each of the three preferences is approximately normally distributed across Western populations. In theory in any group of people you will find all three preferences.

The following exercise will help develop your understanding on this:

SSS Preferences

Most people prefer just one or two of the SSS perceptions (i.e. Sight/Visual – Sound/Hearing – Senses/Kinaesthetic).

Which of the following types of expression most fits your own style?

1. Sight/visual

"That looks good"
"The way I see it"
"I get the picture"

Here the preference is for visual images, and a tendency to remember primarily what is seen. You think mainly in pictures and use mental images for ideas, memory, and imagination. You get angry silently and seething. You doodle when talking or listening. You speak fast. You prefer art to music. You prefer to talk to people face-to-face. You forget names but remember faces. You believe that a picture is worth a thousand words. You learn best from books, writing things down, making mind-map pictures, and watching videos.

2. Sound/auditory

"That sounds good"
"I am all ears"
"I hear what you're saying"

Here the preference is to listen; therefore you are easily distracted by noise, and will remember primarily what has been said. You think in sounds (voices or noises). You prefer lectures to reading. You get angry at an outburst of words. You forget faces but remember names. You prefer to talk to people on the phone. You speak at a medium pace. You prefer music to art.

You learn best from listening to lectures, reading with emotion laden words, by verbally explaining to someone else and listening to audiotapes.

3. Senses/kinaesthetic

"That feels good"
"Hang on in there"
"That touched a raw nerve"

Here the performance is for "hands on" exercises: you remember best what has been done. You represent sounds and stimuli as feelings. You think better when moving. You find it hard to sit still. You get angry by gritting your teeth, clenching fists and then storming off. You prefer to talk to people while you are moving about. You speak at a slower pace. You prefer acting to music and art. You learn best from being "hands on", from playing games, from moving, from making things and from sorting your notes into order (continuously).

Using All Our Influences for Effective Learning

Everyone has a personal learning style. Accommodating this will result in learning that is more effective.

By finding out what our strength is, then we can play to that strength – but remember that if we only use one style, we close off a part of our processing power.

We usually do have a preferred style, but we also need to be aware of all the other styles and other inputs. Then, we can try to widen our perception, especially when in group learning situations. Also, we can then increase our understanding about other people who will likely have different perceptions; we can then perhaps be more in agreement with them.

We can also see that the use of only one of these inputs is a personal weak area, an area for our personal development. Then we can consider correcting the weakness by putting personal effort into those parts of learning which we don't like. To do this will take time and will take effort; things that have not been consciously seen, heard or sensed before will now have to be looked for and opened up.

We can then maximise and increase our processing power.

Key points:

- Recognise that learning is important.
- Make it a conscious process and THINK how you can learn better, (then reconsider and revise and do it)
- Learn about yourself and your learning style/preferences
- Determine if your preferences may be self-limiting
- If so, try to correct these self-limitations
- And continue to build on your existing strengths

Making the Time for Learning

Time is a priority; our learning time must be managed. The following exercise illustrates the main aspects to be considered:

> **Time**
>
> Ask yourself:
>
> - What time of day are you the most alert?
> - What is your daily/weekly study plan?
> - What is the time allowed for breaks? (Most people remember best what is learnt first and last, so more breaks mean more is remembered).

It is important to set a personal timetable for learning. We all have available the same amount of time (there are only 24 hours in a day). Time is the great leveller. Often what separates out successful people from others, is how they use their time.

To create this "extra" time, we can consider the following:

- Get up earlier
- Sacrifice other less important activities
- Stop watching TV
- Work our learning into other activities
- Shorten the lunch hour
- Use train/bus/airline travel time
- Always have learning material with us, so we can dip into it when unexpected opportunity is presented
- Use a diary to plan our time

Consciously planning and controlling the use of our time helps us to keep up momentum.

However we choose to release time for learning, we will need to set some target dates. Deadlines will focus us and force us to manage our time. For example if our learning involves assessments, then we should obviously focus on working towards these dates.

The following Mind Map summarises Time Management in Learning:

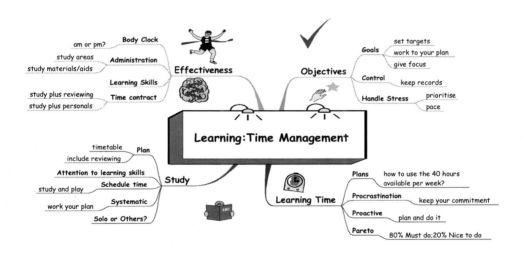

Finding the Right Location

Remember the importance of learning in a friendly atmosphere and comfortable surroundings. When you self study you can directly manage this, so ask yourself the following questions:

Location

- Are the furniture, lighting, and temperature comfortable?
- Will relaxing music help me relax and concentrate?
  (For example, silence is golden for some; for others, background music helps)
- Have I surrounded myself with 'positives?'?
  (For example, trophies, certificates, photographs etc.)
- Have I got all the supplies I need?
  (For example, books, pens, paper, etc.)
- Is it reasonably tidy?
  (For example, having a sense of order with filing, etc.)
- Does it encourage me to learn and to focus?

Sometimes a simple change of location can make a great deal of difference. It is important therefore to discover that which works best for our learning.

Part 4. Learning Skills

There are many useful techniques to help us learn. The most important of these are:

- *Listening.* (Key aspects: Focus – Abbreviate - Review)
- *Memory.* (Key aspects: Chunk it - Review - Review - Review)
- *Note-taking.* (Key aspects: Organised - Format (mind maps?) - Review)
- *Reading.* (Key aspects: Preview - Read (Questions) - Read (Note-take) - Read ("Got it?") - Review (Answer questions) - Review)
- *Writing.* (Key aspects: Group ideas - Loop together by rough draft – Review – Revise – Review – Edit – Rewrite - Evaluate)

It will be seen once again that a common element is reviewing.

Let's look at each of these in more detail.

Listening

Listening plays an important part in learning, whether learning is formal or informal. Listening is an important skill to develop. Listening is not just the natural and passive act of hearing. Listening is more than just hearing. It is about understanding and then translating this understanding into action.

Listening is not an easy skill to learn. Yet its importance is immense. How many times has someone criticised us for not listening?

Always remember when thinking about listening that we have two ears and one mouth. So we should remember to use them in that proportion.

Listening is hard work, which requires concentration. We need to be Active Listeners.

Concentration demands interest. One "trick" to help us is to behave in a way that will help us concentrate, by being prepared, acting interested and getting involved. Don't wait to be "in the mood." Get started and act interested. Often enthusiasm will grow out of our action.

Active listening in a one-to-one situation involves us looking the other person straight in the eye while they are speaking. Listen without interrupting. Absorb what they say. Try really to understand. When they have finished speaking, repeat it back to them by paraphrasing what was said. For example, "so as I understand it, what you said is X". Only when they agree can you move forward.

This shows that we have listened and demonstrates we have heard.

Active and productive listening in a group situation starts by understanding ourselves and then by understanding the listening situation.

Let's expand this further:

1. Get Ready

- Review what you expect, (for example, the notes from any previous learning)

- Eliminate any distractions (for example, uninterested colleagues)
- Anticipate what is being said - you then become active
- Determine why you are there - know why you are listening
- You are there complete - not just the body – but with an active mind to focus on the now and not on yesterdays or tomorrow problems

2. Assume the position

- Sit up, don't slouch – let your posture speak
- Watch as well as listen to body language and to visual aids, etc.
- Acknowledge what you hear by nods and questions as your active involvement completes a feedback loop
- Take notes
- Squarely face the speaker
- Open posture is to be kept by you, as this shows the speaker you are receptive
- Lean slightly forward as this shows your presence and interest
- Eye contact holds interest
- Relaxing shows you are at ease and receptive

3. During the process

- Focus on content and ideas and believe what the person is saying is true for them – do not focus on their appearance/accent/tone/personality – focus on why you are there (presumably this is to gain or refine your knowledge and skills) – focus your attention as you would if you were having a one-to-one conversation with a friend.
- Abbreviate your notes – it is only you who need to understand

them, not anyone else – also, abbreviate your own ideas so you can understand the speakers' ideas!
- Review and revise your notes within 15-20 minutes of the end.

So **READY – SWAT/SOLER - FAR**, is the mnemonic for listening. (Mnemonics are a helpful memory aid!).

Memory

Much of the learning process involves remembering. To retain information we must actively absorb ourselves in a subject. In turn we need to make connections in the brain. These connections require us to repeat and review information ("Use it or loose it"). Much of learning will mean that we have to Review and Review and Review!

Memory is based on the ability to create links and associations between information. The memory is a store that requires recall to access it. Recall is the trigger or key which is needed to open up the store.

These triggers are association techniques: -

- Linking ideas to colours and emotions (for example, angry links to the colour red)
- Pegging ideas to rhymes (for example, I before E except after C)
- Mnemonics or creative sentences (for example, a mnemonic for listening is   "Ready – Swat/Soler – Far", as detailed in the previous section)
- Practising using your memory (for example, practising using visual cues)

- Putting meaning into it (for example, determining your WIIFM)
- Review/Review/Review (for example, immediately in 24 hours, in one week, in 6 months)
- Being healthy (for example, right combination of rest, food, exercising, and a healthy body equals a healthy mind)
- Breaking when studying (for example, maximum 20/40 minutes' heavy concentration, then a 5-minute review – this will help retention, as we remember easier the first and the last parts of a learning session)
- Remembering to remember (by practising remembering)

Remembering to remember is important, because even when we try to remember, we will forget. New information is rapidly lost, especially in the first 20 minutes. 70 to 90% of new information can be easily lost in one day.

So if you are really serious about wanting to remember then you must:

- Review it within 20/30 minutes
- Break long sessions in 20/40 minutes blocks followed by 5-minute reviews
- Remember that reviewing for 20 minutes a day for 5 days is better than reviewing for two hours at one go
- Keep information in bite size chunks of seven items or less (as this suits our short-term memory)

Finally let's try and put all these ideas together in the mnemonic, "STOOR USE":

1. Spread out any heavy memory work (e.g. detailed learning of complicated formula) over several sessions – 20 minutes a day for 5 days is better than 2 hours at one go

2. Test and retest yourself by repeating previous learnt material

3. Organise your material by putting it into patterns or relationships – i. e. the idea of mind-mapping note-taking

4. Over-learn by reviewing material you have learnt several times, as constant repetition does actually work

5. Recite material out loud, – answering questions aloud, improves recall by at least 80 per cent

6. Use all your senses:
    - See it (by reading and visualising)
    - Say it (by reading and hearing)
    - Feel it (by reading and feeling)

7. Study before sleeping and upon awakening – reviewing right before sleep enables you to process while you are sleeping – when you awake then review it again

8. Expect to remember by making it a decision – if you really want to remember, then you will – attitude is your secret weapon – believe in yourself and in your ability to learn, and remember that you do need will to develop a skill

Note-Taking

Note-taking is another personal skill which when learnt will enhance the overall learning process. Notes contain key facts and therefore enhance the recall. Note-taking also ensures you become active in the learning process.

The format of notes kept is often a very personal and individualistic matter. They are kept for us and us alone. Therefore, no two people's notes will look the same. There are, however, some common aspects, as follows:

1. Get organised

- Use a spiral notebook
- Date and number all pages

2. Set up a format – for example:

- Main ideas in the left margin of right-hand page, with recall/review ideas in the right margin – on the left-hand page, write down questions or textbook notes

or
- Mind-mapping with main ideas and branches containing details

3. When taking notes,

- Include all definitions, lists, formulas, or solutions
- Leave plenty of space to allow in-filling with your later ideas/connections
- Use symbols, diagrams, abbreviations

4. If taking notes when listening, it will help if you:

- Listen out for the speaker's voice changes, as this usually signifies important points
- Listen out for any repetition, as this is a clue to the importance of the material
- Stay actively involved
- Ask questions to clarify what is unclear
- Keep on thinking, reflecting, and reacting

5. Review

- Immediately refine any missing areas and rewrite any garbled notes
- File your notes in a logical order/sequence, and build up your personal library

Reading

Reading is a portable, versatile and flexible way to gather information in the learning process.

The key to effective reading is to be mentally active, so we then think about what we read. Remember that reading is thought guided by print. Writing has been the author's job and that job is done. Reading is the learner's job and that job is now ours.

To read effectively it is important to have a system. The following pointers can help:

1. Preview

- Browse the materials to see what's coming

- Plan your reading into 15/20 minute sections

2. Read Once

- Actively ask questions about each section or heading – for example, who, what, when, why, where, how?
- Write down what questions you want answering

3. Read it again

- Actively read not the words, but the ideas
- Engage your senses by reading out loud, underlining the text, colour coding, drawing pictures, etc. – make notes and create interest in what you are reading

4. Read it again

- Actively check you have "got it"

5. Review

- Reread the sections, review your notes, and answer any of the questions

File-Writing

Writing is within us all. It is part of our desire to communicate and tell others. But it is probably the last thing we learnt as a child. First we learnt to listen and then from this to speak. Next we started reading, which then led us finally to writing.

The starting point is to get clear objectives or purpose about our writing. Identify the objectives before starting, which include considering the audience. Who are we writing to? Who is the reader? Clear objectives will give you the focus. Why are you writing and what is the purpose and expected outcome?

There are two main keys to effective writing: Grouping and Looping.

Grouping takes us into getting ideas onto a rough plan. Looping takes us through the actual process of writing.

Grouping

The stages in "Grouping" are all about sorting through our thoughts and ideas and then getting them onto paper. It's like a written "brainstorm", with no judgements, just a paper dump. The steps are:

- Put down the ideas in a box or a circle
- Visualise what you see
- Imagine hearing what someone would say about the ideas
- Feel the subject and write down your feelings
- Expand on these inputs and ideas
- Make connections and link these ideas
- Start to see the content forming
- Experience the delight as the structure starts to form into a rough plan

Looping

We then take this rough plan into the next step, "looping". The steps here are as follows:

- **Rough draft is prepared (from the "Grouping" stage)**

- Review with others
- Revise the draft with the feedback received
- Review again with others
- Edit for spelling, grammar etc.
- Rewrite with final content and with edited changes
- Evaluate

Now all of these steps in looping, (5*R with 2*E), are themselves a Loop – just keep going around the loop until your file or report is finalised and you are happy with the finished article.

Reviewing

The common element in the above learning techniques (listening, remembering, note-taking, reading and writing) is reviewing. Without this, our recall deteriorates ("Use it or lose it"). Practise trying out what you have learned, reflecting on it, talking to others, and going back to the original source of information – these are all review activities.

The following diagram illustrates reviewing:

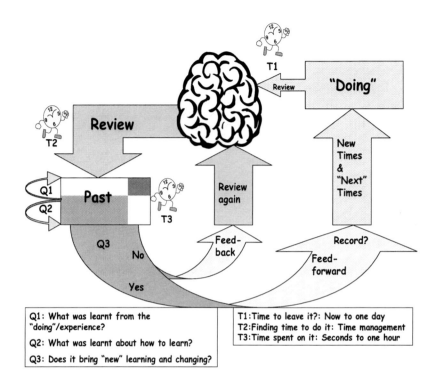

Q1: What was learnt from the "doing"/experience?

Q2: What was learnt about how to learn?

Q3: Does it bring "new" learning and changing?

T1: Time to leave it?: Now to one day
T2: Finding time to do it: Time management
T3: Time spent on it: Seconds to one hour

Reviewing by questioning

- **What?** Look back over events & gather facts objectively
- **So what?** Look at feelings, ideas and opinions
- **Now what?** Look at the future = change and development

Questioning "self"

- Do I respond by habit?
- Do I respond to feedback?
- What are my assumptions?
- How will this affect me?
- How else should I look at this?
- What else could it mean?
- How else can I use this?
- But above all; Ask...ask....ask!

Question asking is a key skill, as noted by the following:

"The problem with Western managers is the emphasis on finding the right answer, rather than asking the right question" (Peter Drucker).

"The mark of a person is in the questions they pose, not just in the statements they make" (Reg Revans)

"The problem is not to find clever people to come up with answers, but to find people who ask good questions" (Reg Revans)

Part 5. The End or Start of learning?

The overall process we have looked can be represented as follows:

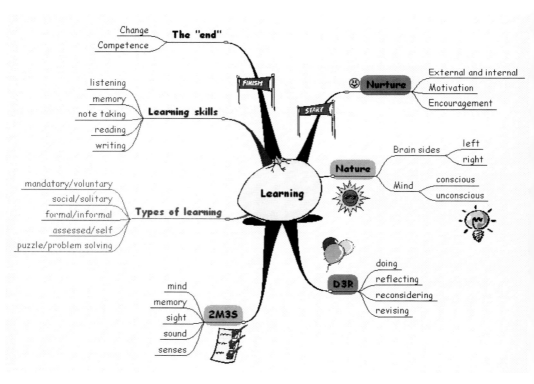

Other Learning Helps

Recognise that learning is similar to physical **exercise** which requires us:

- to be motivated,
- to repeat exercises
- and some times, to stretch beyond what we currently do

Learning and mental exercise require the same steps.

Learning is all about **discovery**. Having this attitude keeps us open to learning. For example:

- Don't try to decide if you like or dislike, agree or disagree – simply look to see what it is – explore it – think and reflect on it – have a go at it
- The discoveries you will then make may be about yourself, the situation, the specific content, or the skill that you're learning
- With this attitude of discovery, then there is something to be learned in every situation
- The more we learn, the more we understand
- The more we understand, then the more we are able to make better decisions about what to change.
- The better the decisions we make, the more successful we are
- The more successful we are, the more we want to learn, and then a learn and change cycle starts again

Remember also the following "helps":

- Commitment to learning (WIIFM)

- Social and self-learning
- Right location or study environment
- Time management
- Mentor support
- Learning log
- Positive, forward-looking attitude

And Finally

Learning how to learn is a skill to be developed. Continuing professional development (CPD) will help you with this skill. CPD will certainly make your learning a conscious process and is covered fully in the Developing People Toolkit.

> "Learning to learn, is often about making the unconscious conscious"

You will know you have been successful with learning when the following position is found

Competence + Commitment = Change.
This involves being personally "Active" in:
- Experience + Exercise
- Positive + Practical
- Emotions + Environment

Think   (Know how)
+Do   (How to)
=Move   (New position)
followed by continual "Active Creation"

Please do not forget the Do's of Learning:

Internal:
- WIIFM=my motivation
- Develop learning skills
- Use cycle Of: doing-thinking-understanding-determining how to.

External:
- Support & Encouragement
- Role Model
- Comfortable place

"I Must":
- "Use it or lose it" : use the total brain power
- Use all of sight/ sound/senses
- Review/review/review
- Be active not passive
- Be creative and do not just consume

"What we think or what we know or what we believe, is in the end of little consequence. The only consequence is what we do" (John Ruskin)

"Those unable to change themselves cannot change what goes on around them" and

"There can be no learning without action" (Reg Revans)

So, finally, what will you now do?

Conclusion

In the introduction we highlighted several areas that managers can work on to improve productivity. These are shown again below with a link, in brackets, to the appropriate Business Toolkit.

- Insufficient planning and control (see the Systems Thinking Toolkit)
- Inadequate supervision (see the Team Management Toolkit)
- Poor morale (see the Motivation Toolkit)
- Inappropriate people development (see the Developing People toolkit)
- IT related problems (included in the Systems Thinking Toolkit)
- Ineffective communication (see the Communication Toolkit)
- Poor Human Resources Management procedures (see the Human Resources Toolkit)
- Poor customer service (see the Customer Service Toolkit)
- Poor training/learning for specific skills and procedures (dealt with in this Learning Toolkit)

Readers are encouraged to take advantage of the complete list of toolkits, which complement each other to provide a comprehensive portfolio of concise pocket guides to improve personal and business performance.